Cake Characters

To Antonella,
With Best Wishes

Annie

ANN PICKARD

Cake Characters

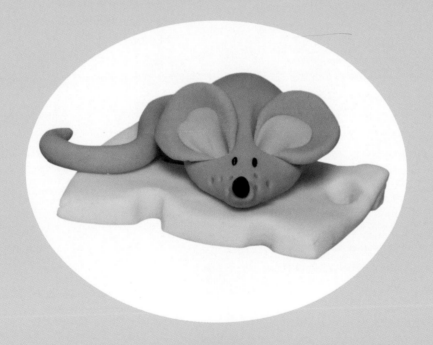

GUILD OF MASTER CRAFTSMAN PUBLICATIONS

First published 2009 by
Guild of Master Craftsman Publications Ltd
Castle Place, 166 High Street,
Lewes, East Sussex BN7 1XU

Reprinted 2010

Copyright in the Work © GMC Publications Ltd, 2009

ISBN: 978-1-86108-643-3

A catalogue record of this book is available from
the British Library.

Associate Publisher: Jonathan Bailey
Production Manager: Jim Bulley
Managing Editor: Gerrie Purcell
Project Editor: Gill Parris
Managing Art Editor: Gilda Pacitti
Designer: Rob Janes

Set in Gill Sans

Colour origination by GMC Reprographics
Printed and bound by Kyodo Nation Printing Co.

Why we love cake characters

ALL THESE HAPPY LITTLE CHARACTERS are so simple to make, they can be made by adults or children – just make them for fun and place on an iced board or use them to decorate a cake for someone you love.

You can make your models weeks or months in advance, ready to decorate your Christmas or birthday cakes. Just remember not to store them anywhere damp!

Because no moulds or cutters are used, each little character you make will have its own personality and no two will be identical.

You can use any modelling medium, not just sugarpaste. Use salt dough to make big models or coloured modelling clay to make tiny models. Just increase or decrease your Guide to Sizes chart (see page 133).

The possibilities are endless – do have a go – and have fun!

 1

 2

 3

 4

Contents

1 Teddy	10	5 Ducks	26
2 Elephant	14	6 Frog	30
3 Rabbits	18	7 Mouse	34
4 Penguins	22	8 Small dogs	38

 5

 6

 7

 8

 **9**

 **10**

 **11**

 **12**

9	Sheep	42
13	Large dog	58
10	Pig	46
14	Tiger	62
11	Cat	50
15	Lion	66
12	Monkey	54
16	Pony	70

 **13** **14**

 **15**

 **16**

 **17**

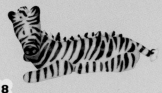 **18**

 **19**

 **20**

17 Donkey 74

18 Zebra 78

19 Crocodile 82

20 Mole 86

21 Snowman 90

22 Santa Claus 94

23 Eskimo 98

24 Polar bear 102

 **21**

 **22**

 **23**

 **24**

25 Woman in chair 106

26 Man in chair 110

27 Toddler 114

28 Baby 118

29 Clown 122

30 Mechanic 126

Techniques 130

About the author 152

Dedication and Acknowledgements 152

Suppliers 153

Index 154

Everyone loves teddy bears and this little character would look great on any cake for children, whatever the occasion. Make him smooth like a new bear, or fluffy like an old, worn bear.

Teddy

Materials

Sugarpaste in 'Teddy', black or brown (see pages 138–39)

Piece of uncooked spaghetti

Black paste food colour and cocktail stick or toothpick

Modelling tool

Part	Template	Colour
Body	A	Teddy
Feet	2 × E	Teddy
Head	C	Teddy
Arms	2 × E	Teddy
Nose	G	Black or brown
Nose tip	J	Black or brown
Ears	2 × G	Teddy

See templates for sizes on page 133

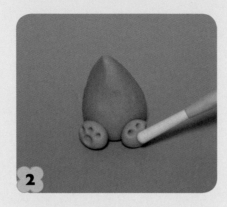

1 Body Form the ball for the body into a cone shape, using 'Teddy' colour sugarpaste.

2 Feet Using one round ball of the same colour for each foot, press on to the base of the body – use a little brushed-on water to secure if necessary. Mark each foot three times along the top of the foot with the point of the tool, and once with the round end of the tool.

3 Arms Form a long teardrop shape for each arm (the arms should reach two thirds of the way down the body), stick each from the very top of the cone.

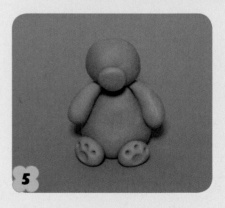

4 Head Place a piece of raw spaghetti down in to the body and break it off ½ in (12mm) above the icing. Place the round head firmly down on to the body, the head should cover the top of the arms.

5 Nose Press a small, slightly squashed ball of icing in to the lower half of the head.

6 Tip of nose Press the tiny ball in black or brown on to the top of the nose.

7 Ears Make 2 x ⅕ in (5mm) holes in top of head with pointed end of tool, squash each ball flat, pinch one side of it to a point, push the point firmly in to the ear hole, repeat with other ear. Push the pointed end of tool in to each ear to firmly secure.

8 Eyes and mouth Mark eyes with black paste colour on the end of a cocktail stick (see 'How to mark eyes', page 143). Paint on a little mouth.

Ruffled texture

Use a cocktail stick to mark the surface of the teddy and make it look ruffled or fluffy.

Blanket

To make a blanket for your teddy, roll out 2oz (60g) of pale-coloured sugarpaste, ⅛ in (2–3mm) thick, cut out a small oval, mark the edges with a knife and paint on little flowers or dots.

Elephants are always a favourite model to go on a cake.
For variety, make them in different shades of pink and different sizes,
and lay some on their tummies or backs.

Elephant

Materials

Sugarpaste in pink (see pages 138–39)

Piece of uncooked spaghetti

Black paste food colour and cocktail stick or toothpick

Modelling tool

Part	Template	Colour
Body	A	Pink
Feet	2 x E	Pink
Arms	2 x E	Pink
Head	C	Pink
Ears	2 x E	Pink

See templates for sizes on page 133

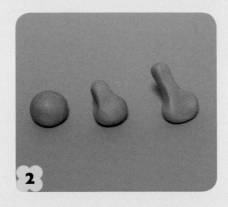

1 Body Follow stages 1–3 of Teddy (see page 12) but don't mark the toe details on each foot.

2 Head Shape the sugarpaste into a pear shape and gently pull and stretch the thinner end to form the trunk.

3 Trunk Place a short piece of spaghetti into the body, break it off with ⅕in (5mm) showing, place on the head, make a hole up the end of the trunk and mark little lines all the way along with a knife.

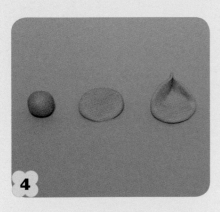

4 Ears Squash each ball flat until it is ⅘in (2cm) in diameter and pinch one side to form a point.

5 Earhole Make a very large hole at the side of the head and push in the ear point, push the pointed tool in to the centre to secure. Repeat the stages for the other ear.

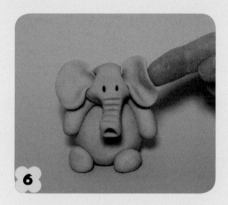

6

7

6 Ears and eyes Push the middle of the outer ear gently inwards on both sides. Mark the eyes (see 'How to mark eyes', page 143).

7 Tail Mark a hole in the bottom if your elephant is lying down, form a little tail and push the point in securely.

Other ideas

For an adult celebration add some little champagne bottle candles and small plastic glasses.

Cut several thin strips of tearing ribbon and curl them with the blade of a knife or scissors, arrange these around or between the elephants.

The blue rabbit could be made in any colour you like and placed on your cake with a teddy or duck to keep him company. Your other bunny will look great in a garden scene.

Rabbits

For both: black paste food colour, cocktail stick or toothpick, piping bag (see page 144) and green royal icing (see page 145)

Materials – Blue rabbit

Blue, white, brown and orange sugarpaste (see pages 138–39)

Part	Template	Colour
Body	B	Dark blue + white
Feet	2 × F	Dark blue + white
Arms	2 × E	Dark blue + white
Tummy	F	White
Head	Large D	Dark blue + white
Nose	H	Brown
Tail	E	White

Materials – Brown rabbit

Brown, black, white and orange sugarpaste (see pages 138–39)

Part	Template	Colour
Body	B	Dark brown
Front legs	E	Dark brown
Head	D	Dark brown
Tail	F	White
Nose	I	Black

See templates for sizes on page 133

Blue rabbit

1 Body Follow steps 1–3 for Teddy (see page 12), but mix a light blue sugarpaste.

2 Tummy Squash ball of white sugarpaste into a fat cone shape and flatten. Using a little brushed-on water to stick, press on to the rabbit's tummy.

3 Fluffy tummy Use a cocktail stick to blend the edges of the white tummy into the blue.

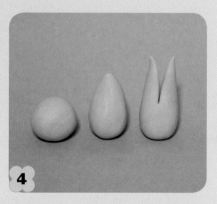

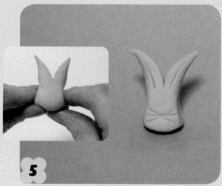

4 Head Using light blue sugarpaste, shape the head ball into a pointy cone shape, cut through the top of the cone to form two long ears.

5 Ears Place your thumbs under the rabbit's head and your fingers above it; flatten the base of the head and the ears will move slightly apart, as shown above. Mark up each ear and the whiskers with a knife.

6 Tail and face Turn the rabbit around and place a cone-shaped tail under his bottom; mark it with a cocktail stick to make it look fluffy. To complete the face, add a little brown ball for the nose insert (see large dog, stage 6, page 60). Mark the eyes (see 'How to mark eyes', page 143).

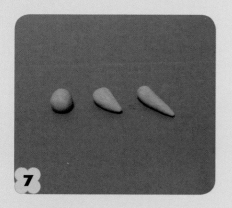

7 Carrots Form several little carrots from orange sugarpaste, mark lines on them with knife and pipe green leaves at the top – see 'Making royal icing for piping' (page 145). Tuck one carrot under the rabbit's arm.

Brown rabbit

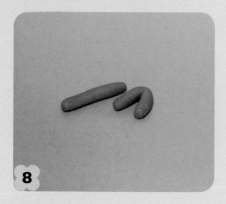

8 Front legs Shape the brown sugarpaste into a sausage shape 1in (2.5cm) long, bend it around into a 'C' shape.

9 Body and tail Make a cone-shaped body, place the tapered end over the curve of the legs. Add a fluffy tail – see stage 6.

10 Head Make the head following stages 4–6 of Toy rabbit (see facing page). Mark the eyes (see 'How to mark eyes', page 143). Add three little lines at the end of each foot for toes.

These little penguins are quick and simple to make and can be placed on a Christmas cake for a lovely seasonal scene. Why not add some little white Christmas trees, too!

Penguins

Materials

White, black and orange sugarpaste (see pages 138–39)

Black paste food colour and cocktail stick or toothpick

Modelling tool

Part	Template	Colour
Large penguin		
Body	A	White
Feet	F x 2	Orange
Beak	G	Orange
Small penguin		
Body	D	White
Feet	G x 2	Orange
Beak	H	Orange

See templates for sizes on page 133

1 Body Form your cone from the ball of sugarpaste, the top should be rounded not pointed.

2 Feet Shape each orange ball into a teardrop shape and place them next to each other in a heart shape.

3 Add feet Pick up the body and place it on the back of the feet, slide the body towards you and feet will attach.

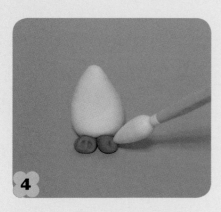

4 Mark toes Using the pointed end of the modelling tool, firmly impress three times on each foot.

5 Cut triangle Roll out a small piece of black sugarpaste to a thickness of ⅛in (2–3mm), cut a triangular shape 2in (5cm) long. Very lightly brush the middle of the triangle with a little water.

6 Stick on back Stick the black triangle to the back of the white cone with the shortest side of the triangle at the base. Bend the top of the triangle over the penguin's head.

7

7 Hole for beak Push a deep hole in to the penguin's face just below the black point.

8

8 Add beak Form a small ball of orange into a double pointed shape – push one end into the hole in the face. Mark the eyes (see 'How to mark eyes', page 143).

9

9 Baby penguins Make some baby penguins following exactly the same method but with smaller balls of sugarpaste.

10

10 Ice From a block of white sugarpaste cut some angular pieces of icing of various sizes for your pieces of ice.

This colourful little duck is the easiest character to make in the book. It would look at home in a pond scene with a group of ducks on a blue cake and piped grass around the sides.

Ducks

Materials

Yellow, red and brown sugarpaste (see pages 138–39)

Black paste food colour and cocktail stick or toothpick

Pieces of uncooked spaghetti

Modelling tool

Part	Template	Colour
Large duck		
Body	B	Yellow
Head	D	Yellow
Beak	Small G	Red
Wings	2 × F	Yellow
Small duck		
Body	E	Yellow
Head	F	Yellow
Beak	H	Red

See templates for sizes on page 133

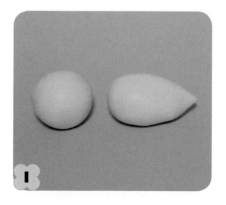

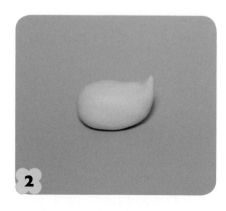

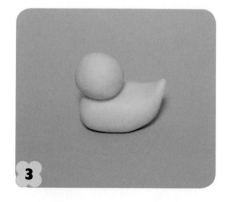

1 Body Form the ball for the body into a fat cone shape.

2 Tail Gently bend the end point upwards to form the tail.

3 Head Stick the round ball for the head on to the fat end of the cone, use a little brushed-on water to secure if necessary.

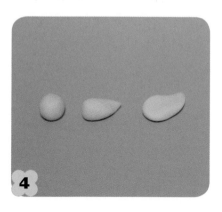

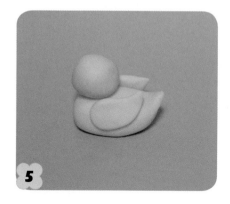

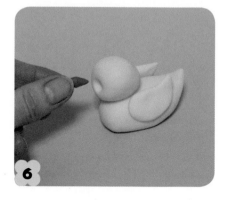

4 Wings Make two small balls, form each one into a teardrop shape, then bend the point upwards and flatten each one.

5 Join wings Using a little brushed-on water to secure, stick one wing to each side of the body.

6 Beak Form the red ball for the beak into a long diamond shape, then make hole in the face and push in one point firmly.

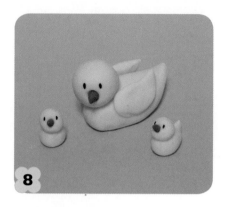

7 Eyes Add long eyes to the duck, marked with black paste colour on the end of a cocktail stick (see 'How to mark eyes', page 143).

8 Baby ducks Make a few baby ducks ready to go on your 'pond' – there is no need to add wings to the baby ducks.

9 Bulrushes Roll some small pieces of brown sugarpaste into a cylinder shape, push short lengths of raw spaghetti up into each one – ensure the spaghetti is different lengths.

10 Grass Following instructions for 'Piping hair and grass' on page 145, pipe green grass spikes around the base of the bulrushes.

One little cheeky frog can be placed on a rock for a lovely design.
Make some extra baby frogs or, for a bit of fun, some pairs of eyes only,
peeping out of the water.

Frog

Materials

Green, white, black and grey sugarpaste (see pages 138–39)
Piping tube
Modelling tool

Part	Template	Colour
Large frog		
Body	A	Green
Legs	2 x D	Green
White eye	G	White
Black eye	I	Black
Small frog		
Body	C	Green
Legs	2 x E	Green
White eye	H	White
Black eye	J	Black

See templates for sizes on page 133

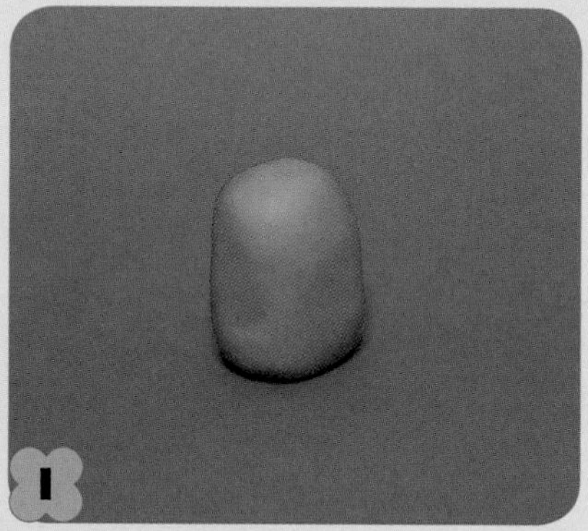

1 Body Shape the body ball into a short oval. Press it down firmly onto your work surface to flatten the base.

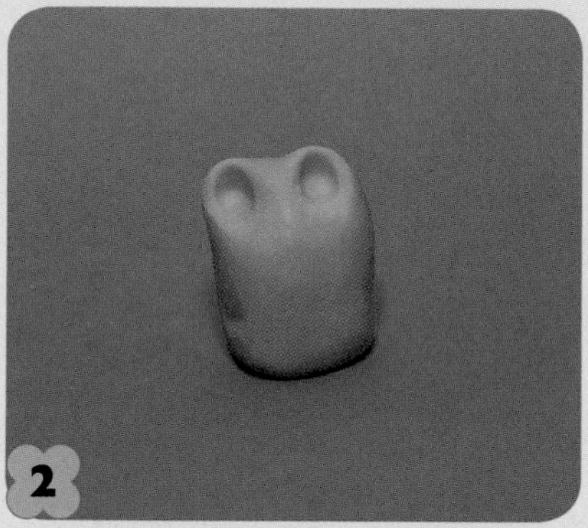

2 Face Mark indents for eyes using the rounded end of your modelling tool, push each indent upwards.

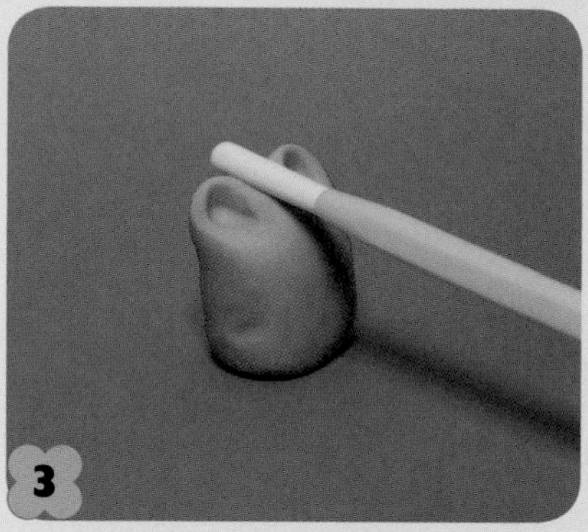

3 Face Push the rounded end of the tool down between the eye indentations.

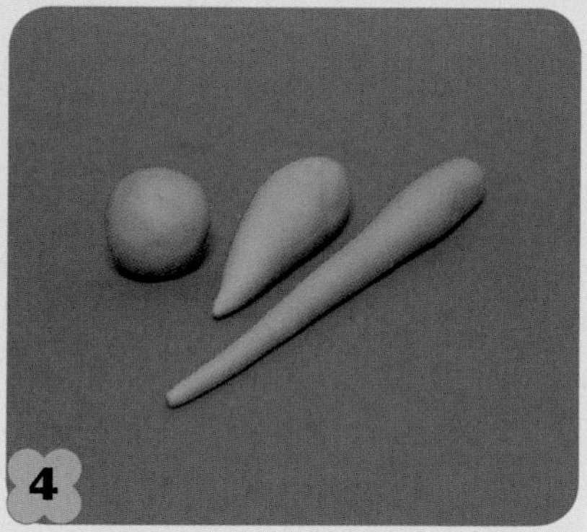

4 Legs Shape each ball into a cone and then elongate until they are 3in (7.5cm) long.

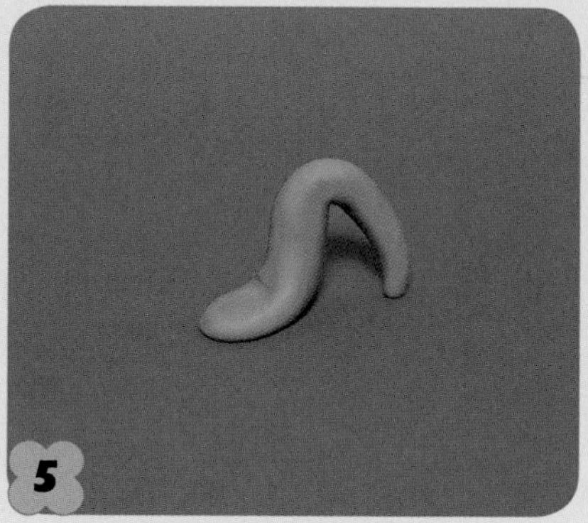

5 Leg Flatten the fattest end for the foot and bend the remaining length of the leg up and down.

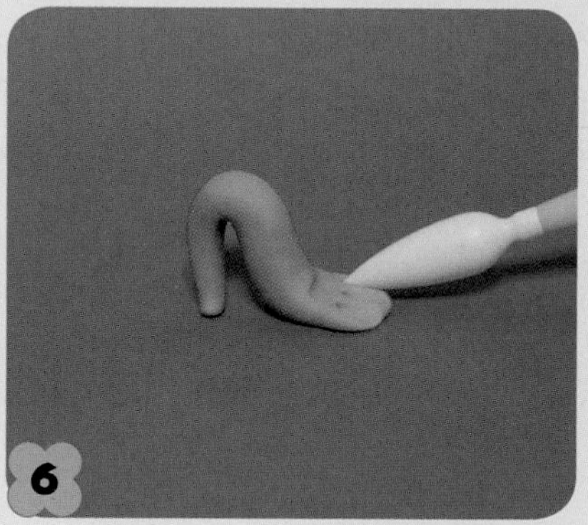

6 Toes Use the pointed end of the modelling tool to mark three dents (four toes).

7 Add legs Stick one leg each side of the body, use a little brushed-on water to hold firmly in place.

8 Eyes Squash the white balls flat and stick one in each of the indentations. Squash the black balls and stick on the bottom of each white ball.

9 Smile Make a smile using the large open end of a small stainless steel piping tube, press in one side firmly.

10 Rocks and pebbles Make grey sugarpaste pebbles in various shapes and sizes. Large flat ones would be suitable for your frog to sit on.

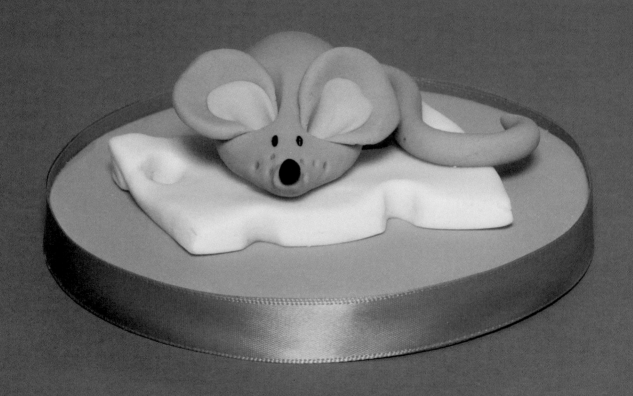

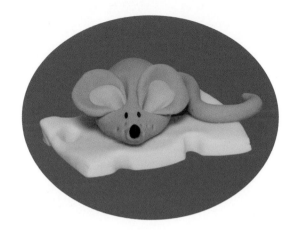

These little icing mice can be made in white or grey sugarpaste and, for a dinner party surprise, why not put them all over your cheeseboard at the end of the meal?

Mouse

Materials

Sugarpaste in grey, pink, black and yellow (see pages 138–39)
Black paste food colour and cocktail stick or toothpick
Modelling tool

Part	Template	Colour
Body	A	Grey
Ears	2 x E	Grey
Inner ear	2 x G	Pink
Nose	I	Black
Tail	E	Grey

See templates for sizes on page 133

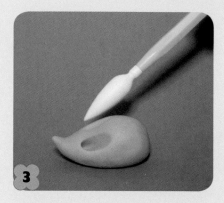

1 Body Form the round ball of grey sugarpaste into a cone shape.

2 Nose Bend the tip of the mouse's body up for the nose.

3 Ears Rest the pointed tool along the back of the mouse and push the end in to make two large holes.

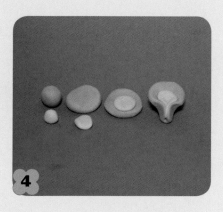

4 Squash the grey ball, press on the squashed pink ball, flatten together and then pinch one side to a point.

5 Push the point of each ear into the big holes.

6 Push the pointed end of the tool into each ear to firmly stick it in place.

7 Nose Form a little teardrop shape from the black ball and push it into a hole in the mouse's nose.

8 Eyes Mark the eyes with black paste colour (see 'How to mark eyes', page 143) then, with a clean cocktail stick, make little whisker holes each side of the nose.

9 Tail Form your tail into a long tapering sausage shape. Place one end under the mouse and curl the tail.

10 Cheese Roll out a very pale yellow thick wedge of sugarpaste, make some big holes in it and push in a few indentations around the side.

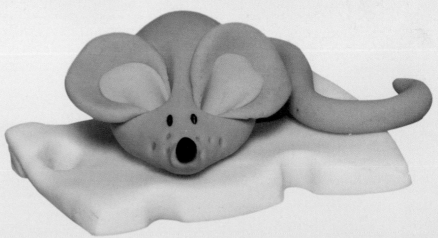

Both these dogs are made using the same technique, but look how just a few changes can make such different results. Don't forget to add a little ball for them to play with!

Small dogs

Materials – Brown dog

Chestnut brown and black sugarpaste (see pages 138–39)
Black paste food colour/cocktail stick or toothpick/modelling tool

Part	Template	Colour
Feet	4 x F	Chestnut brown
Body	A	Chestnut brown
Head	D	Chestnut brown
Nose	H	Black
Long ears	2 x F	Black
Tail	G	Black

Materials – White dog

White and black sugarpaste (see pages 138–39)
Black paste food colour/cocktail stick or toothpick/modelling tool

Part	Template	Colour
Feet	4 x F	White
Body	A	White
Head	D	White
Nose	H	Black
Short ears	2 x G	White
Tail	G	White

See templates for sizes on page 133

Brown dog

1 Feet Form the four feet into round balls and place in a square ¾in (19mm) apart.

2 Body Make the body into an oval shape and press it firmly down on top of the feet. Make a dent with your finger where the head is to be positioned.

3 Head Shape the head into a pear shape and place – using water if necessary to stick – on to the indent.

4 Nose Mark a little hole for the mouth and above it make a much deeper hole for the nose; insert a teardrop-shaped black sugarpaste nose.

5 Long ears Form two ears from black sugarpaste. Make two long thin cone shapes, flatten and stick one on each side of the head. Mark eyes (see 'How to mark eyes,' page 143).

6 Tail Form a long tail shape with a point at each end, make a hole at the end of the dog's body, stick the tail in firmly and curl the end up.

White dog

7

7 Body and head Repeat steps 1–4 and stage 6 with the white sugarpaste, but make the head slightly more square.

8

8 Ears Squash each ear into a long oval, flatten slightly and stick the lower third of each one to the sides of the head, securing them with a little brushed-on water.

9

9 Short ears Bend the top part of each ear downwards. Mark the eyes (see 'How to mark eyes', page 143). Also add two tiny dots above the eyes for the eyebrows.

10

10 Fluffy body Use a cocktail stick and pull out the icing all over the body to create a rough fluffy look.

Little woolly sheep will always be a hit for adults and children alike. Place a little fence around them and ice your cake in green for a summer meadow scene.

Sheep

Materials

White and peach sugarpaste (see pages 138–39)

Black paste food colour and cocktail stick or toothpick

Piping bag with 'star' tube (see page 144)

White royal icing (see pages 145)

Part	Template	Colour
Body	A	White
Head	Small D	Peach
Ears	2 × H	Peach
Feet	4 × F	White

See templates for sizes on page 133

1 Body Using white sugarpaste follow stages 1–2 of Brown dog (see page 40).

2 Head Stick a little cone-shaped peach-coloured head on the indent of the body – stick with a little brushed- on water.

3 Ears Make two little teardrop-shaped ears and stick one on each side of the head.

4 Nose and eyes With a cocktail stick make two holes at the end of the face and mark the eyes (see 'How to mark eyes', page 143).

5 Wool Using a piping bag with a small star tube, pipe royal icing 'blobs' or stars all over the sheep for wool, then pipe a higher group of blobs on top of the head in between the ears.

Pigs are always popular. Make these fat little characters and arrange in some brown royal icing 'mud'. For a lovely farmyard scene, add some baby piglets, too.

Pig

Materials

Pale pink sugarpaste (see pages 138–39)

Modelling tool

Black paste food colour and cocktail stick or toothpick

Part	Template	Colour
Feet	4 x F	Pale pink
Body	A	Pale pink
Head	D	Pale pink
Nose	F	Pale pink
Ears	2 x G	Pale pink
Tail	G	Pale pink

See templates for sizes on page 133

1 Body and legs Follow stages 1–2 of Brown dog instructions (see page 40), but using pale pink sugarpaste.

2 Head Place the round ball on to the dent in the body. Press on firmly to secure or use a little brushed-on water. Squash the smaller nose ball and press in on to the head.

3 Nostrils Mark the two holes with the pointed end of your modelling tool.

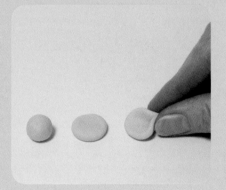

4 Ears Make the ears (see right) and attach them to the top of the head with the points sticking upwards, then bend the point downwards.

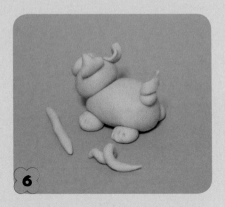

5

6

5 Eyes When both your ears are in position you can mark the eyes with black colour (see 'How to mark eyes', page 143). You may need to push the ears back up whilst marking the eyes.

6 Tail Turn your pig around and make a deep hole in the bottom, form a long tapered sausage, push one end into the hole and twist the remaining tail into a curly shape.

This little cat can be used in so many scenes.
Make some tiny mice to accompany it, have it sleeping in an armchair,
or even on the lap of your man or woman figure.

Cat

Materials

Grey, white, pale pink and black sugarpaste (see pages 138–39)

Black paste food colour and cocktail stick or toothpick

Piping bag (see page 144)

Pink royal icing (see page 145)

Part	Template	Colour
Legs	2 x E	Grey
Body	B	Grey
Head	D	Grey
Face	G	White
Nose	J	Black
Tail	F	Grey

See templates for sizes on page 133

1 Legs Roll each ball into a sausage shape 1½in (4cm) long bend them around.

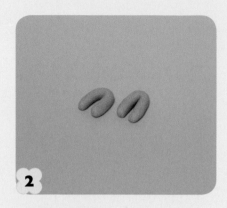

2 Bend legs Place the four legs next to each other with the toes all pointing to the side.

3 Body Form the ball into a short sausage shape and stick it over the curved part of the legs.

4 Head Pinch two ears at the top of the ball of sugarpaste. Use a cocktail stick (toothpick) to indent each ear.

5 White face Squash the ball of white icing and then flatten it on to the lower part of the cat's head.

6 Black nose Shape the little black nose into a triangular shape and press it on to the top of the white patch.

7 Eyes and whiskers Mark the black eyes (see 'How to mark eyes', page 143) then use a cocktail stick to impress three whiskers on each side of the face.

8 Toes and tail Shape the ball into a long tapered sausage shape, curve it and place one end under the cat's bottom. Use the tip of a cocktail stick to make your cat a little fluffy. Mark three lines on each foot.

9 Balls of wool Shape a few round balls and place them around your cat.

10 Piping wool Make some pink royal icing. Half fill a small piping bag, cut a straight hole at the end of the bag and pipe some wool around the balls and some long trailing bits as well.

Your cheeky monkey can be part of a jungle scene.
Why not make a family group all lounging around, eating bananas and leaning
on each other? Some could even be lying on their bellies or backs.

Monkey

Materials

Teddy brown, dark brown, white and yellow sugarpaste
(see pages 138–39)
Modelling tool
Black paste food colour and cocktail stick or toothpick

Part	Template	Colour
Rock	A and B	Black and white (mixed)
Body	A	Teddy brown
Legs	2 × D	Teddy brown
Arms	2 × E	Teddy brown
Tail	E	Teddy brown
Head	D	Teddy brown
Nose	F	Teddy brown
Nostrils	H	Sand
Ears	2 × G	Teddy brown
Banana	F	Yellow

See sugarpaste templates for sizes on page 133

1 Rock and body Form a large rock shape, squash slightly. Make the body cone shaped and place on top of the rock.

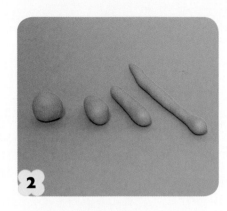

2 Arms and legs Form the legs and arms as illustrated.

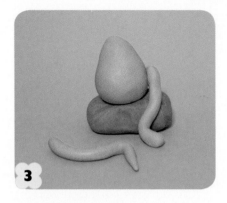

3 Legs Join the legs to the body as shown and bend the feet back. Secure with a little brushed-on water.

4 Arms Taper the top of the arms and stick to the shoulders. Use a cocktail stick (toothpick) to mark three toes at the end of each limb.

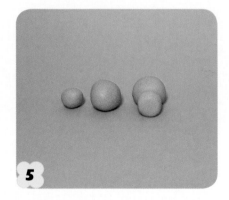

5 Head and nose Form the two balls, stick them to each other (the larger ball is the top of the head, the smaller the nose).

6 Nostrils Squash the sand sugarpaste into an oval, then flatten and press it on to the lower section of the head. Push two holes into the little nose you've added.

7

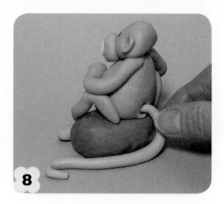

8

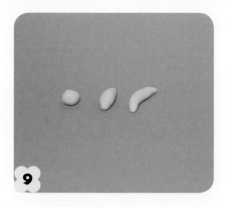

9

7 Head and ears Place the head on to the body with a piece of spaghetti to support it. Add the ears (see Teddy step 7, page 13). Mark the eyes (see 'How to mark eyes', page 143).

8 Tail Form the ball of icing for the tail into a long sausage shape. Insert one end into a hole at the back of the monkey.

9 Banana Form a little banana from each ball of sugarpaste.

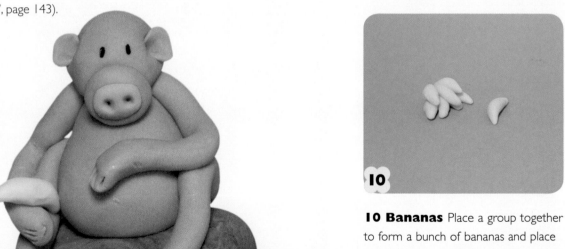

10 Bananas Place a group together to form a bunch of bananas and place one in the monkey's hand.

Just a few little changes and you can make this into a variety of dogs. Scratch his surface to make him fluffy, or make in white and paint on black spots for a Dalmatian.

Large dog

Materials

Sand and black sugarpaste (see pages 138–39)

Piece of uncooked spaghetti

Black paste food colour and cocktail stick or toothpick

Modelling tool

Part	Template	Colour
Body	A	Sand
Legs	4 × E	Sand
Head	D	Sand
Tail	F	Sand
Nose	H	Black
Ears	2 × G	Sand

See sugarpaste templates for sizes on page 133

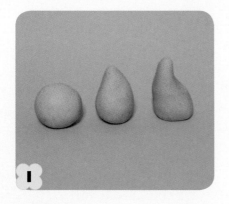

1 Body Form the body into a cone shape then pinch the top to one side.

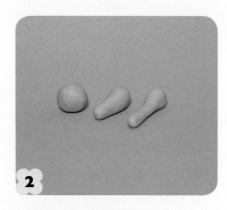

2 Attaching back legs Form each back leg into a fat sausage shape, thin one end.

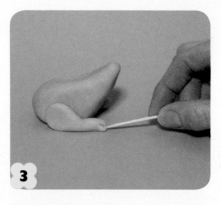

3 Back legs Squash each leg to the side of the base of the dog.

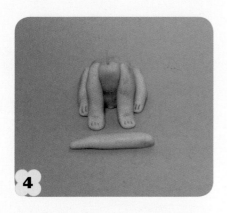

4 Front legs Form each leg into a cone shape, the height of the dog's body and stick them to the front of the body with a little brushed-on water.

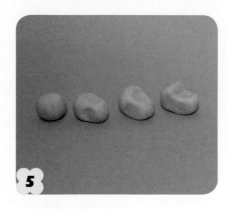

5 Head Form the ball into the shape illustrated.

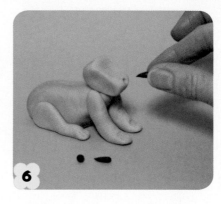

6 Nose Place a piece of spaghetti into the body with a little showing above the neck. Place on the head. Form a little black teardrop-shape nose, insert into a hole.

7 Ears Form each ear into a long oval shape; squash flat and, using a little brushed-on water, stick the bottom half of an ear to either side of the head.

8 Ears and eyes Bend the top of the ears downwards. Mark the eyes (see 'How to mark eyes', page 143).

9 Tail Form the tail into a tapered sausage shape. Make a hole in the body and insert one end into the hole; curve the end of the tail.

10 Furry coat Use a cocktail stick (toothpick) to gently scratch over the joins. Also scratch little areas on the dog's body. Add a ball or bone to your final scene if you wish.

This lovely lazy tiger is having a rest on a log.
You could also surround him with lots of bright green piped grass
and place him directly on your cake, as if he's hiding in a jungle.

Tiger

Materials

Orange, white, black and dark brown sugarpaste
(see pages 138–39)
Modelling tool
Black paste food colour and cocktail stick or toothpick
Fine paintbrush

Part	Template	Colour
Body	A	Orange
Legs	4 x E	Orange
Head	D	Orange
Tail	F	Orange
Nose	F	White
Nose tip	H	Black
Ears	Small G x 2	Orange
Tree trunk	A and B	Dark brown

See sugarpaste templates for sizes on page 133

Note:
If you wish your tiger to lie on the tree trunk, follow steps 9 and 10 first, then make the model on top.

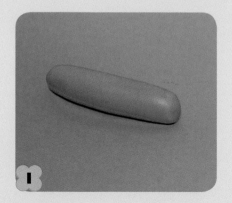

1 Body Form your body into a sausage shape 4in (10cm) long.

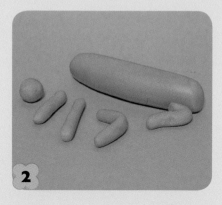

2 Legs Roll each leg into a sausage shape 1½in (4cm) long, bend each into a 'V' shape and stick one leg to each corner of the body.

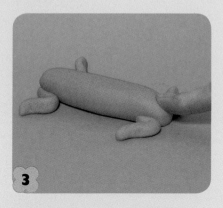

3 Neck Use your finger to make a dent at the neck of the tiger. This will enable his head to face upwards.

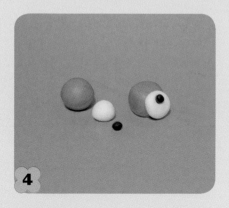

4 Head Form the three balls of icing, join the orange and white balls, squash together to stick, make a hole at the top of the white ball and insert a black teardrop-shaped nose-tip.

5 Ears Follow instructions for Teddy ears, step 7 (page 13), to complete the head.

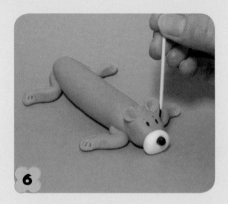

6 Eyes and toes Add eyes to the head (see 'How to mark eyes', page 143). Mark three toes at the end of each foot.

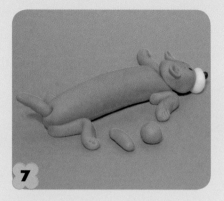

7 Tail Form a 1½in (4cm) long tail. Make a deep hole in the bottom of the tiger and push the tail in firmly.

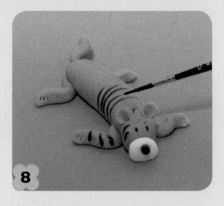

8 Stripes Dilute your black paste colour with a little water and, using a fine-quality brush, paint the stripes all over the tiger, from the bottom upwards.

9 Tree trunk Form a large flat sausage shape – cut one end straight and the other end so that it slopes downwards.

10 Branches Cut a few little branches and scratch the surface of the 'bark' roughly.

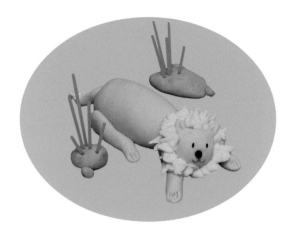

This cuddly lion is resting in the sun, hiding behind the long grass. Make another lion, but leave off the piped mane and you have a cute lioness to keep him company.

Lion

Materials

Sand and black sugarpaste (see pages 138–39)

A piece of uncooked spaghetti

Black paste food colour and cocktail stick or toothpick

Piping tube

Piping bag (see page 144)

Pale yellow royal icing (see page 145)

Part	Template	Colour
Body	A	Sand
Legs	4 x E	Sand
Head	D	Sand
Tail	H	Sand
Nose	I	Black

See templates for sizes on page 133

I Body Follow Large Dog steps 1–4 (see page 60) but push the front of the body down so it's resting on your work surface.

2 Head Form a cat's head (see Cat stage 4, page 52). Mark eyes (see 'How to mark eyes', page143). Make a hole for the nose and push in a teardrop-shaped piece of black sugarpaste.

3 Tail Make a small sausage shape for the tail and push into a hole in the bottom.

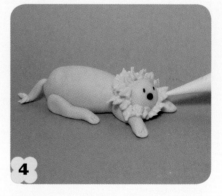

4 Mane Mix up some pale yellow royal icing and follow 'piping' instructions (see page145). Pipe lots of little spikes of hair all around the head and at the end of the tail. Paint two little curves under the nose in black.

5

Tip

You could pipe long spikes of grass all around your lion, too (see 'piping hair and grass', page 145).

5 Pebbles and grass

Form some little pebbles, flatten slightly and stick in some short spaghetti pieces to represent long grass.

Create your pony on a green field with a fence around.
You could add a few sheep for a farm scene, or add hay bales made from
little shredded breakfast cereals in groups around your pony.

Pony

Materials

Chestnut brown sugarpaste (see pages 138–39)

Piece of uncooked spaghetti

Modelling tool

Black paste food colour and cocktail stick or toothpick

Piping bag (see page 144)

Chestnut brown and green royal icing (see page 145)

Red sugarpaste, for flowers

Small blossom cutter

Chocolate sticks for fence

Part	Template	Colour
Body	A and C	Chestnut brown
Legs	4 x E	Chestnut brown
Tail	G	Chestnut brown
Head	D	Chestnut brown

See templates for sizes on page 133

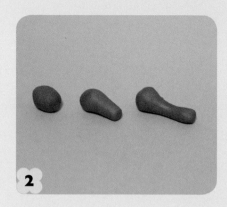

1 Body Form a sausage shape 4in (10cm) long. Make the neck end thinner and the bottom fatter, bend the neck up.

2 Legs Shape each ball into a cone then a hambone shape – round at one end and thinner at the other.

3 Attaching the legs Join the legs to the body; use a little brushed-on water to stick in place. Place spaghetti down into the neck.

4 Head Form the head shape.

5 Ears Pinch the ears up at the top of the head, making them quite high and pointed.

6 Nose and eyes Place the head on the body. Mark a line up each ear with a cocktail stick. Mark the eyes (see 'How to mark eyes', page 143) and two holes for the nostrils.

7

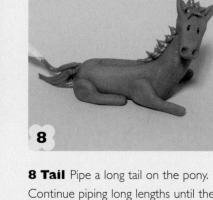

8

9

7 Mane Follow piping instructions on piping (pages 144–45), using a small paper bag half-filled with chestnut-brown royal icing.

8 Tail Pipe a long tail on the pony. Continue piping long lengths until the required thickness is achieved.

9 Fence Make your Pony on a green-covered board or cake. Form a fence around the 'field' with chocolate sticks. Hold them in place with some piped green grass.

10

10 Flowers Cut some small flower/blossom shapes, press the centres in slightly to cup them and stick them around the fence posts.

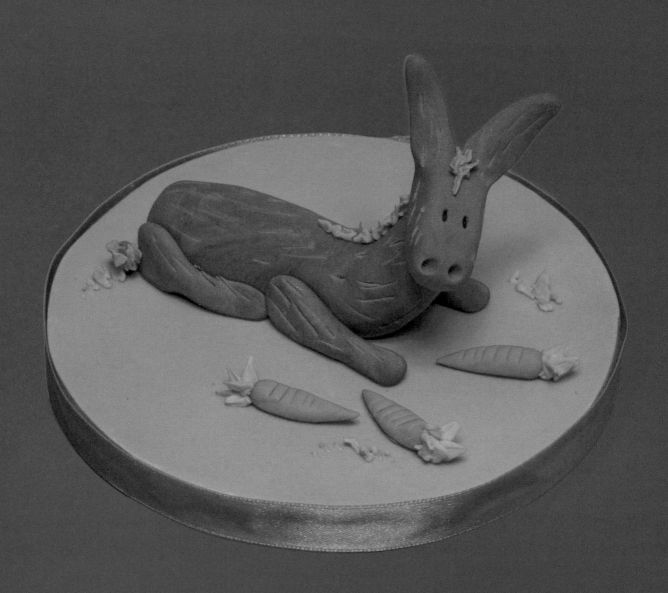

This lovely donkey could be part of a summer beach scene on a pale yellow cake, or you could place him on a Christmas cake with a few little Christmas trees all around.

Donkey

Materials

Mid-brown sugarpaste (see pages 138–39)

Modelling tool

Black paste food colour and cocktail stick or toothpick

For the carrots: orange sugarpaste, piping bag (see page 144) and green royal icing (see page 145)

Part	Template	Colour
Body	A and C	Mid-brown
Legs	4 x E	Mid-brown
Tail	G	Mid-brown
Head	Large D	Mid-brown

See templates for sizes on page 133

1 Body and legs Follow Pony stages 1–3 (see page 72), but make the neck slightly shorter. Make a thin sausage tail for the donkey, insert into a hole. Insert a piece of spaghetti into the neck, to support the head.

2 Head Form the head ball into a long pointed cone, bend the pointed end upwards for the ears.

3 Ears Cut through the top of the cone to divide it evenly and form ears.

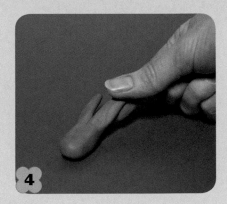

4 Ears Twist each ear outward so that the flat part is facing the front and pinch flat. Push both the ears forward.

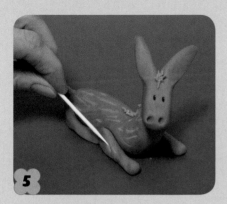

5 Add head Place the head on the body, with the raw spaghetti to support it. Mark the eyes (see 'How to mark eyes', page 143). Mark the nostrils and pipe the mane (see Pony stages 6–7, pages 72–3).

Form some little carrots to place on your final scene (see Rabbits stage 7, page 21).

This super zebra is a very similar shape to the pony and donkey
– just change the ear shape and paint all over with black stripes.
Place him on a lime green background for dramatic effect.

Zebra

Materials

White sugarpaste (see pages 138–39)

Piece of raw spaghetti

Black paste food colour and cocktail stick or toothpick

Piping bag (see page 144)

White royal icing (see page 145)

Small, good-quality paintbrush

Part	Template	Colour
Body	A and C	White
Legs	4 × E	White
Tail	G	White
Head	D	White

See templates for sizes on page 133

1

2

3

1 Body and neck Follow Pony Step 1 (see page 72), but make the neck shorter.

2 Legs Form each leg into a cone, then a hambone shape – round at one end and thinner at the other. Join the legs to the body with a little brushed-on water.

3 Head Form your head following Pony stages 4–6 (see page 72), but round the tops of the ears instead of making them long and pointed. Mark eyes and nostrils.

4 Mane and tail Pipe the mane on the zebra in white royal icing (see piping techniques, pages 144–45). Form a little sausage tail, insert into a hole and pipe a tuft of hair at the end.

5 Stripes Paint stripes all over the zebra with the paintbrush and black paste colour.

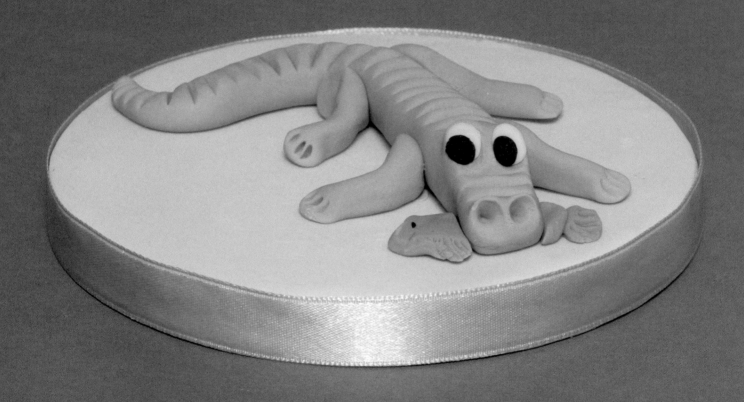

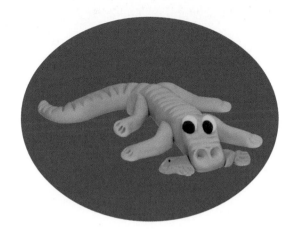

Have a go at making this unusual model.
Your snappy crocodile could be in a blue river, or climbing up
the riverbank having caught a fish for tea!

Crocodile

Materials

Green, white, black and light blue sugarpaste (see pages 138-139)

Quilting tool (pointed end)

Modelling tool

Black paste food colour and cocktail stick or toothpick

Part	Template	Colour
Body	A and B	Green
Legs	4 × E	Green
Eye white	H	White
Eye black	J	Black
Fish body	G	Light blue
Fish tail	I	Light blue

See templates for sizes on page 133

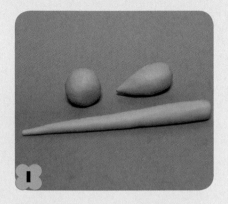

1 Body Mix balls A and B together, start to shape a cone and then elongate it until it is 7in (17.5cm) long.

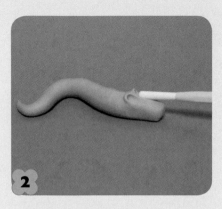

2 Eye sockets Push up two big eye sockets at the fat end, 1½in (4cm) in from the end.

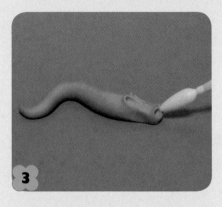

3 Nostrils Push in two smaller indentations right at the end of the face.

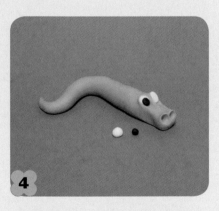

4 Eyes Add the eyes, made from a squashed ball of white and a smaller ball of black on top.

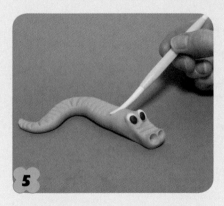

5 Ribbing Using the pointed end of the quilting tool mark deep lines all the way along the nose of the crocodile and right down the back and tail.

6 Legs and feet Form four fat, drumstick-shape legs; impress three times at the end of each foot for the toes.

7 Attaching the legs Add the four legs to the body and bend them all out slightly. Stick with water if necessary.

8 Fish Form the two little parts for the fish body and a little triangular tail.

9 Fish tail Mark the fins and tail with lines using the pointed end of the quilting tool.

10 Hungry crocodile Cut the fish in half and place on each side of the crocodile's mouth.

Moles are such cute little characters. This cheeky one is popping out of the ground to say 'Hello'! Make lots of mounds of sugar all round him for more molehills all over your green cake.

Mole

Materials

Dark brown and black sugarpaste (see pages 138–39)

Cocktail stick or toothpick

Apricot glaze (see page 136)

Modelling tool

Soft brown sugar

Part	Template	Colour
Body	B	Dark brown
Eyes	2 x J	Black
Paws	2 x E	Dark brown
Nose	I	Black

See templates for sizes on page 133

1 Body Form the body into a fat cone shape. Place it firmly down and bend nose forward.

2 Ears With the round end of the tool press two little indentations into the mole's head for the tiny ears.

3 Eyes and nose Make two holes for the eyes and another hole in the tip of the nose. Form the three balls into teardrop shapes and insert them into the holes.

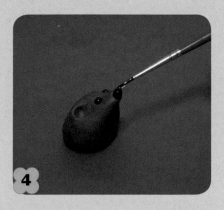  

4 Add sparkle Paint a little apricot glaze on to the eyes and nose to give them a sparkle.

5 Skin Scratch the body all over with a cocktail stick to give a slight furry texture to the mole.

6 Paws Form each paw into a flat triangular shape.

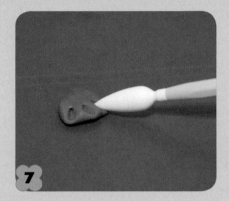

7 Impress the paws Impress deeply three times on each paw using the end of the tool.

8 Form the claws Now mark deeply with a cocktail stick in between each of the previous three impressions and pull outwards to make little claws.

9 Add earth Place your mole on your cake or iced cake-board and surround with a generous quantity of soft brown sugar to resemble a mound of earth.

10 Add the paws Push the paws into the 'earth' on each side of the body. Piped 'grass' could be added, too (see page 145).

This is an easy character to make. When you've finished him you can place the hat on his head, or tuck it under his arm. Sprinkle him with 'snow' icing sugar and form lots of little snowballs.

Snowman

Materials

White, red, dark brown and orange sugarpaste
(see pages 138–39)
Piece of uncooked spaghetti
Black paste food colour and cocktail stick or toothpick
Modelling tool
Icing sugar

Part	Template	Colour
Body	A	White
Arms	E	White
Scarf	2 x F	Red
Head	D	White
Hat	Small D	Dark brown
Nose	G	Orange

See templates for sizes on page 133

1 Body Form the white sugarpaste body into a cone shape.

2 Arms Make two long teardrop-shaped arms and stick them to each side of the body, using water to secure if necessary.

3 Scarf Squash a ball of red sugarpaste flat, place it over the top of the body.

4 Scarf Stick a piece of spaghetti down into the body, break off with a little showing. Add second piece of scarf with little lines marked along straight end.

5 Nose hole Make a very deep hole for the nose in the midde of the face.

6 Nose Shape the orange ball into a long double-pointed diamond shape (see inset above). Push one half of the diamond into the hole.

7 Eyes Mark eyes with black colour and cocktail stick (see 'How to mark eyes', page 143).

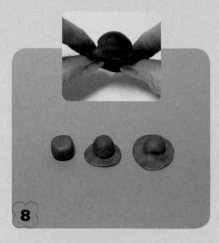

8 Hat Pinch a brim all around the hat by squeezing the edges whilst revolving it (see inset above).

9 Placing the hat Place the hat under the arm of your snowman as an alternative to placing it on his head.

10 Snowballs Form lots of round snowballs in various sizes and sprinkle with icing sugar.

Children and adults alike will love this character.
Make Santa in a snowy scene waiting for his reindeer.
Some little green trees around him could complete the scene.

Santa Claus

Materials

Red, black and flesh sugarpaste (see pages 138–39)
Modelling tool
Black paste food colour and cocktail stick or toothpick
Piping bag (see page 144)
Small star tube
White royal icing (see page 145)

Part	Template	Colour
Body	A	Red
Belt	F	Black
Feet/shoes	2 × F	Black
Arms	2 × E	Red
Hands	2 × G	Flesh
Head	D	Flesh
Nose	I	Flesh
Hat	D	Red

See templates for sizes on page 133

1 Body and belt Form a cone shape body in red sugarpaste. Form a sausage for the belt, squash it and wrap around the body – use a little brushed-on water to secure if required.

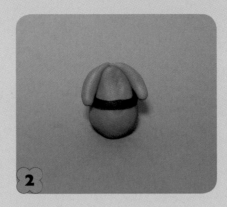

2 Arms Add two cone-shaped arms. The arms should reach to just over halfway down the body.

3 Shoes Form two black teardrop shapes and place together. Place body firmly on back of feet.

4 Armholes Make the holes in the end of the arms with the pointed end of the modelling tool.

5 Hands Shape little teardrop-shaped hands and push one up each sleeve, pinch the hands slightly to flatten.

6 Head and ears Place a piece of spaghetti into the body to support the head. Push the round head on to it. Mark two indents for the ears.

7 Nose Form a teardrop-shaped nose, make a hole in the face and push the nose in.

8 Eyes and hair Mark two oval eyes with two tiny dots above for eyebrows (see 'How to mark eyes', page 143). Pipe white royal icing hair from a star tube (see inset above, and piping instructions on pages 144–45).

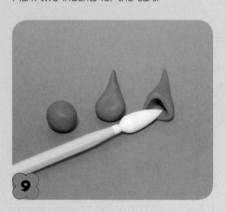

9 Hat Shape a very pointed cone shape hat, pushing the pointed end of the tool into the hat to open it up.

10 Bobble Pipe royal icing around the base of the hat and a bobble on top.

This cute eskimo is about to make his igloo, so remember to cut lots of little blocks out of icing for him. You could also make a few baby penguins to join him in his snowy scene.

Eskimo

Materials

Dark blue, black and flesh sugarpaste (see pages 138–39)

White and orange royal icing for piping

A piece of uncooked spaghetti

Black paste food colour and cocktail stick or toothpick

Small, good-quality paintbrush

Paper piping bag (see page 144)

Small star piping tube

White and orange royal icing (see page 145)

Part	Template	Colour
Body	A	Dark blue
Arms	2 x E	Dark blue
Feet	2 x F	Black
Hands	2 x G	Flesh
Head	D	Flesh
Nose	I	Flesh
Hood	C	Dark blue

See templates for sizes on page 133

1 Body Follow Snowman stages 1–2 (see page 92) for the body and arms.

2 Feet and hands Follow stages 3, 4 and 5 of Santa Claus (see page 96).

3 Head and nose Place a piece of spaghetti into the body leaving some sticking out to support the head. Place on a round head. Make a hole in the centre and add a teardrop-shaped nose.

4 Eyes and hair Mark the eyes (see 'How to mark eyes', page 143). Paint on a black fringe with black food colour. Mark a little hole for the mouth.

5 Hood Squash the ball until it is 2in (5cm) in diameter. Brush a little water on to the back of the head and stick on the hood.

6 Hood Bend over the top of the hood – it should overhang the fringe.

7 Piping fur on hood Push the two sides of the hood into the sides of the face. Using royal icing and a star tube, pipe fur around the hood (see piping instructions, pages 144–45).

8 Piping on costume Pipe two thin lines of orange in a zig-zag along the front of the eskimo.

9 Blocks of snow Cut lots of little cubes of ice to arrange around the eskimo.

This chilly polar bear is fishing for his tea.
Add a few more bears around the ice hole and they could be having a fishing party! A snowman or eskimo could also be fishing in this scene.

Polar bear

Materials

White, black and blue sugarpaste (see pages 138–39)

A piece of uncooked spaghetti

Black paste food colour and cocktail stick or toothpick

Small piece of bendy flower wire

Part	Template	Colour
Body	A	White
Legs	2 × E	White
Arms	2 × E	White
Head	D	White
Ears	2 × G	White
Nose	I	Black
Reel	2 × G	Black

See templates for sizes on page 133

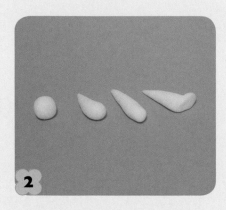

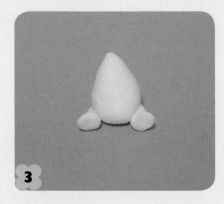

1 Body Form the body into a cone shape.

2 Form legs Form each leg into a large cone shape, bend the fat end upwards and pinch it to form a foot.

3 Attach legs Brush a little water on each side of the bottom of the cone body and stick each leg into place.

4 Arms Each arm is a cone shape. Stick one on each side of the body, bending the hands around the front so that they almost meet.

5 Head Place a piece of uncooked spaghetti down into the body. Form a short cone-shaped head and place it on top of the body.

6 Ears Make two ⅕in (5mm) holes at the top of the head, follow instructions for Teddy's ears, step 7 (see page 13).

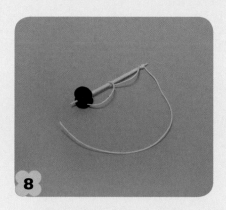

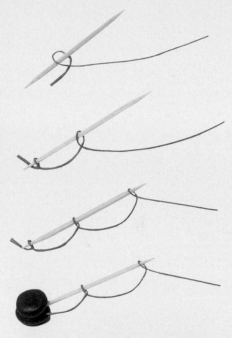

7 Eyes and nose Mark the eyes (see 'How to mark eyes', page 143). Make a hole in the very end of the nose, form the black nose into a teardrop shape and push it into the hole firmly.

8 Fishing rod Use a piece of bendy flower wire and a cocktail stick to form the fishing rod (see right). Squash the two black balls on each side.

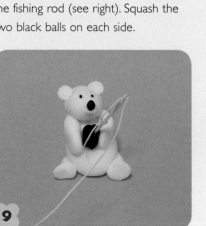

9 Fishing rod Push the fishing rod into the bear's tummy and press the arms in to touch it each side.

10 Fish Form some little blue fishes (see Crocodile steps 8 and 9, page 85) to place on your final scene. Cover your board or cake with very pale blue and cut a hole in it, push a round ball of dark blue into the hole and position the end of the wire into the 'fishing hole'.

Sit your lady in her comfy chair. Change the colours
of her clothes and hairstyle if you wish, and why not make
a little cat or dog to sit by her?

Woman in chair

Materials

Flesh, red and black sugarpaste (see pages 138–39)

A piece of uncooked spaghetti

Black paste food colour and cocktail stick or toothpick

Piping bag (see page 144)

Light yellow royal icing (see page 145)

Part	Template	Colour
Legs	1 × D	Flesh
Skirt	Roll out C	Red
Body	D	Black
Neck	F	Flesh
Arms	2 × large F	Black
Head	Large E	Flesh
Nose	J	Flesh
Hands	2 × H	Flesh
Shoes	2 × small G	Black

See templates for sizes on page 133

Note:
See instructions for making an armchair on page 149. It must be made at least 24 hours before the figure.

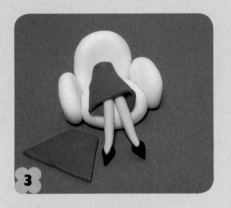

1 Legs Shape your ball of sugarpaste into a sausage 5in (12.5cm) long, bend in half and stick to the base of your armchair; pinch the end of each leg into a point.

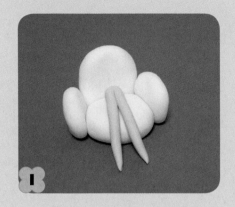

2 Shoes Form each little shoe by shaping the balls into pointed cone shapes, flatten each one slightly and place under each pointed foot, squash together to join.

3 Skirt Roll out the ball of icing, cut the shape shown 4in (10cm) along the base and 2in (4cm) along the top. Place over the top of the legs and fold the edges under.

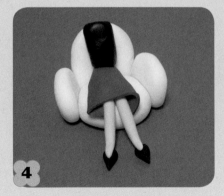

4 Body Form the body into a rectangular shape, then pinch in slightly to taper at the waist. Position on the back of the skirt resting against the back of the chair.

5 Arms and hands Form the arms and hands (follow Baby steps 5–7, on page 120–21). Flatten the palms slightly by pressing them down on to the chair arms.

6 Neck Form the neck shape, pinch the bottom into a 'V' and stick on the body. Push a bit of spaghetti down into the neck, through the body and into the chair.

7 Head Shape the head into an oval, pinch a chin at the base and push in so that the chin slopes up to the back of the head. Place the head down on to the spaghetti at the angle shown above.

8 Facial features Mark the ears, add nose (see Baby stages 8 and 9, page 121). Mark the black eyes (see 'How to mark eyes', page 143) and paint a smile.

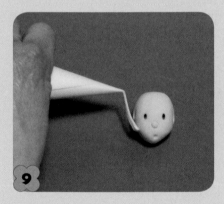

9 Hair Using light yellow royal icing pipe the lady's hairstyle (see piping women's hair, page 148).

Make your man resting in his chair. You could paint on little horizontal lines for sleeping eyes and don't forget to change the hairstyle and colour to match the person you are giving it to.

Man in chair

Materials

Light blue, dark blue, black, flesh and white sugarpaste (see pages 138–39)

A piece of uncooked spaghetti

Black paste food colour and cocktail stick or toothpick

Fine paintbrush

Piping bag (see page 144)

Brown royal icing (see page 145)

Part	Template	Colour
Legs	1 × large B	Dark blue
Shoes	2 × F	Black
Body	B	Dark blue/white mixed
Arms	2 × E	Flesh
Sleeves	2 × F	Dark blue/white mixed
Neck	Small E	Flesh
Head	D	Flesh
Nose	H	Flesh
Newspaper	Roll out C	White

See templates for sizes on page 133

Note:
See instructions for making the armchair on page 149.
The armchair must be made at least 24 hours before the figure.

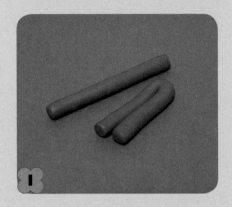

1 Legs Form a long sausage shape 5in (12.5cm) long. Bend in half and stick to the base of your armchair with a little brushed-on water.

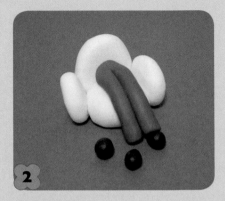

2 Shoes Form each ball into a teardrop shape and stick under the end of each leg.

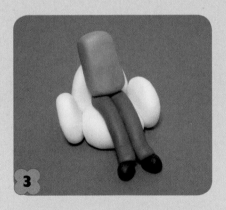

3 Body Form a rectangular shape and stick on to the top of the legs, so it rests against the back of the chair.

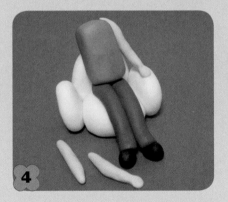

4 Arms Form each arm into a tapered sausage shape 2in (5cm) long, squash the end flat and pinch in the wrist.

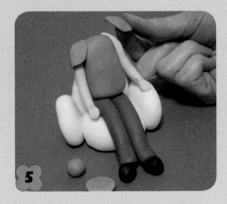

5 Sleeve Flatten the ball for the sleeve, brush a little water at the top of the arm and squash on the sleeve top.

6 Neck Form the little neck shape and place it at the top of the T-shirt, push a piece of spaghetti down into the neck and all the way through the body into the chair.

7 Head Shape an oval head and place on the neck. For the ears and nose follow Baby steps 8–9 (see page 121). Mark the eyes (see 'How to mark eyes', page 143) and paint a smile.

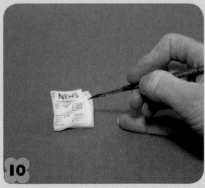

8 Hair Pipe the man's hair with brown royal icing (see piping men's hair, on page 146).

9 Newspaper Roll your white sugarpaste out thinly and cut two rectangles, fold one over and place on the other piece, then fold that over.

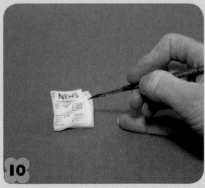

10 Newspaper print Dilute a little black paste colour with some water and paint using a fine paintbrush.

This little toddler could be sitting on an armchair or even his mum or dad's lap. Remember to give him some toys to play with, too, but do make them as tiny as possible.

Toddler

Materials

Blue, brown, red and flesh sugarpaste (see pages 138–39)

A piece of uncooked spaghetti

Black paste food colour and cocktail stick or toothpick

Modelling tool

Quilting tool

Piping bag (see page 144)

Pale yellow royal icing (see page 145)

Part	Template	Colour
Legs	1 × small D	Blue
Shoes	2 × small G	Dark brown
Body	Small D	Red
Arms	2 × small F	Red
Hands	2 × I	Flesh
Collar	G	Red
Head	E	Flesh
Nose	J	Flesh

See templates for sizes on page 133

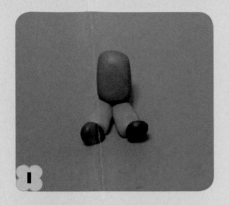

1 Body, legs and shoes Follow 'Man in chair' stages 1–3 (see page 112) but do not place in armchair.

2 Arms and hands Form a long cone shape for the arm, stick one on each side of the body, make a teardrop-shaped hand and insert into the hole at the end of the sleeve.

3 Jumper Place a piece of spaghetti down into the body. Texture the surface of the jumper by rolling the quilting tool gently all over it, horizontally and vertically.

4 Collar Slightly squash the little ball of sugarpaste and place it down on to the piece of spaghetti.

5 Head and ears Form the head into an oval shape, then push it down on to the piece of spaghetti. Mark the ears each side of the head with your modelling tool.

6 Nose Form the little nose into a teardrop shape, make a hole in the face and push the nose into it.

7 Mouth and eyes Impress a little round hole for the mouth. Mark the eyes with black paste colour (see 'How to mark eyes', page 143).

8 Hair Colour some royal icing a pale blonde colour – half fill a small piping bag, and start to pipe the hair (see piping men's hair, page 146). Continue piping the royal icing hair until the hairstyle is complete.

9 Toy Make a selection of little toys to place next to the toddler. Follow the Teddy and Duck instructions (see pages 12 and 28) but make them much smaller.

This cuddly baby could be made on a little blanket, or lying on his back, holding a little teddy bear or duck. The colour of the playsuit could be changed, if you wish.

Baby

Materials

Blue and flesh sugarpaste (see pages 138–39)

A piece of uncooked spaghetti

Modelling tool

Black paste food colour and cocktail stick or toothpick

Fine paintbrush

Part	Template	Colour
Body	A	Dark blue/white mixed
Arms	2 × small E	Dark blue/white mixed
Head	D	Flesh
Nose	I	Flesh
Hands	2 × small G	Flesh

See templates for sizes on page 133

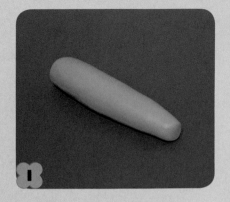

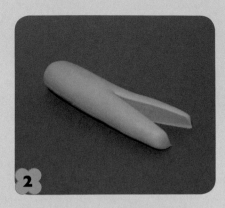

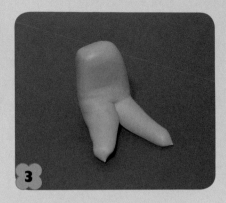

1 Body Shape the ball into a 3in (7.5cm) sausage shape – slightly taper one end to make it thinner.

2 Body Cut evenly lengthways into the sausage at the thinner end, cut it in about 1½in (4cm).

3 Legs Pick up each leg and twist it inwards, bend the other end of the sausage up from the middle to sit your baby up.

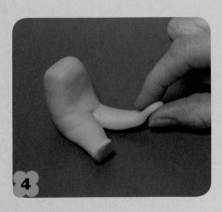

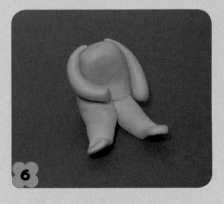

4 Feet Pinch and stretch the end of each leg to make the feet. Bend each foot upwards.

5 Arms Form each arm from a ball of blue sugarpaste pulled into a long, coned shape.

6 Attaching arms Stick on each arm with the pointed end at the top of the shoulders, curve one arm in across the tummy.

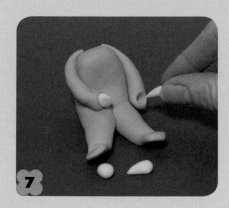

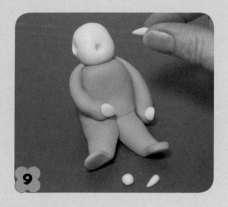

7 Hands Make a hole at the end of the sleeve with the pointed tool, insert a teardrop-shaped piece of sugarpaste for the hand and when it is firmly in place, squash the palm flat.

8 Head Place a piece of spaghetti down into the body, place on an oval head and mark the ears gently with the end of the tool.

9 Nose Form a little teardrop shape, make a hole in the middle of the face and insert the nose.

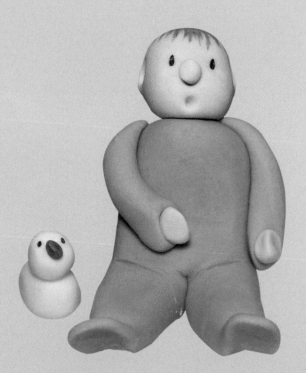

10 Hair Mark eyes (see 'How to mark eyes', page 143). Make a little hole for the mouth. Paint the hair on the baby with a fine paintbrush. You could add a little yellow duck to your final scene (see page 28)

Make your clown as bright and cheerful as possible.
Don't forget to add lots of different-sized juggling balls and
put some in his hands, as well as all around him.

Clown

Materials

Yellow, blue, light blue, red and flesh sugarpaste
(see pages 138–39)

A piece of uncooked spaghetti

Modelling tool

Quilting tool

Black paste food colour and cocktail stick or toothpick

Fine, small paintbrush

Medium carnation cutter

Piping bag (see page 144)

Orange royal icing (see page 145)

Part	Template	Colour
Body	Large A	Yellow
Arms	2 × small D	Yellow
Hands	2 × G	Flesh
Head	D	Flesh
Nose	Small G	Red
Shoes	2 × E	Light blue
Buttons	3 × I	Red

See templates for sizes on page 133

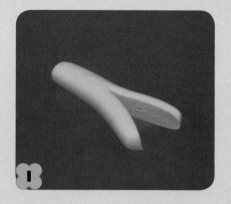

1 Body Form the large ball into a sausage 5in (12.5cm) long – cut lengthways up half the sausage.

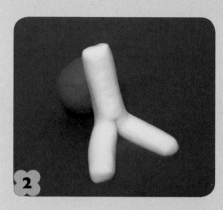

2 Body Twist each leg inwards and sit your clown against a large bright ball of coloured sugarpaste.

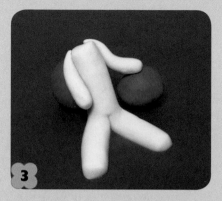

3 Arms Form two arms (see Baby step 5, page 120) and stick the arms to the body with a little brushed-on water. Rest one of the arms on a smaller bright ball.

4 Hands Insert each teardrop-shaped hand into a hole at the end of the sleeve, then flatten each hand slightly.

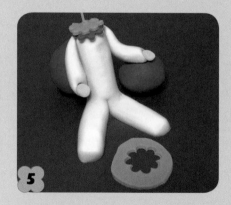

5 Ruffles Roll out two small pieces of blue sugarpaste quite thinly, then cut out two ruffles using a medium carnation cutter. Place them both on the top of the shoulders and push a piece of spaghetti in ready to put the head on.

6 Head Add an oval head, mark ears, add a big red nose (see Baby steps 8–9, page 121). Mark the eyes (see 'How to mark eyes', page 143).

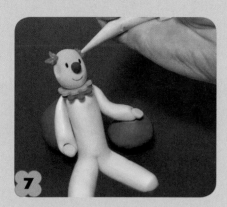

7 Hair and smile Paint a big smile on the face with a fine paintbrush and black colour diluted with water. Pipe the hair with bright orange royal icing (see pages 144–46).

8 Feet Form two bright shoes – mould the ball into a pear shape and stick on the end of the leg with a little brushed-on water to secure.

9 Seams Using the little wheel on the quilting tool, run it up the arms and down the legs right up the front of the outfit.

10 Buttons Give your clown three bright buttons up the front of his suit and secure with a little brushed-on water. Make additional little blue juggling balls in different sizes.

You'll love making little people and this model is suitable for anyone who loves fixing their car. You could add a little toy car in the right colour to complete the scene.

Mechanic

Materials

Dark blue, flesh, dark brown, lilac, yellow, black and grey sugarpaste (see pages 138–39)

A piece of uncooked spaghetti

Black paste food colour and cocktail stick or toothpick

Fine paintbrush

Crimper

Modelling tool

Quilting tool

Piping bag (see page 144)

Brown royal icing (see page 145)

Part	Template	Colour
Tyre	A	Black
Hub cap	2 × G	Grey
Body	Large A	Dark blue
Arms	2 × small D	Dark blue
Hands	2 × G	Flesh/little brown (mixed)
Collar	F	Dark blue
Head	D	Flesh/little brown (mixed)
Nose	H	Flesh/little brown (mixed)
Socks	2 × F	Lilac
Boot Base/Top	2 × E	Dark brown

See templates for sizes on page 133

1 Tyre Squash the ball a little flat for your tyre.

2 Add the treads Use a crimper to pinch the pattern of the tread all around the outer rim, then crimp all around the top of the tyre too.

3 Hub cap Squash the little grey ball on to the middle of the tyre. Make one big hole in the centre of the tyre, then lots of little holes all around with a piece of spaghetti.

4 Body Follow Clown steps 1–4 (see page 124) but using dark blue sugarpaste. Also mark seams on clothing (see Clown stage 9, page 125).

5 Collar Squash a ball for the collar, cut a little triangle out of it and place it on the neck of the mechanic. Push a piece of spaghetti into the body ready for the head.

6 Head Form an oval head, add ears and nose (see Baby stages 8 and 9, page 121).

7 Socks Squash a ball of paste on to the end of each leg. Make lines all around the sock with the edge of a knife.

8 Boots Form one of the balls of brown into a pear shape and the other into a cylinder shape. Join the two together to form a boot.

9 Eyes and hair Mark the eyes (see 'How to mark eyes', page 143) and pipe the hair (see page 146). Paint a smile and tiny dots for eyebrows.

10 Cloths Make some yellow cloths to add to the scene and paint some black 'oil' on the mechanic's boilersuit.

Techniques

How to make fun cake characters!

Sugarpaste templates

If you are a beginner, practise making a duck and teddy before you make one of the more complicated models. Always use the templates below for all your animals and people, as this will save you having to guess the size of each body part.

All the models in this book have been made with bought sugarpaste/rolled fondant icing. I have used Regalice throughout. If you use a different brand, ensure that it isn't too sticky or too elastic in texture.

Method

Each time you create a part of your model, roll it into a smooth ball in the palm of your hands. The warmth of your hands will soften the paste and remove any lines or cracks from its surface. Now match the ball to the correct size ball on the chart.

A

B

C

E

F   G   H

I   J   K

Tip

If your instructions say to use a 'Small A' size, form a ball that fits well inside the outline. Alternatively a 'Large B' would cover the outer rim of the circle.

Equipment for models

Only a few basic tools are required to create the characters in this book and they can all be bought from your local sugarcraft supplier.

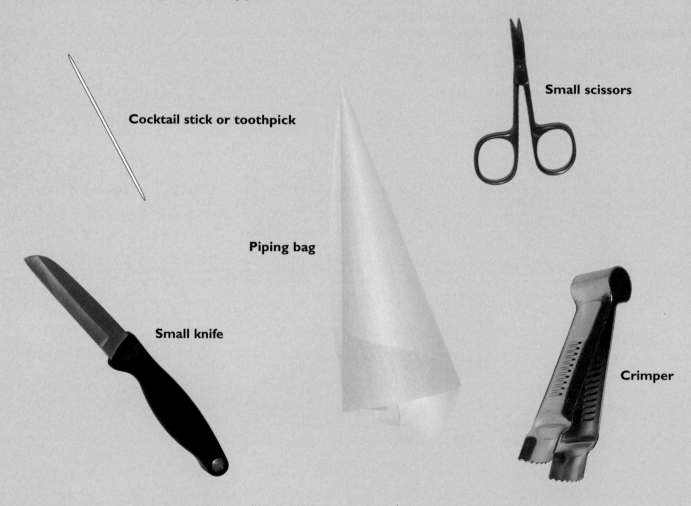

Cocktail stick or toothpick

Small scissors

Piping bag

Small knife

Crimper

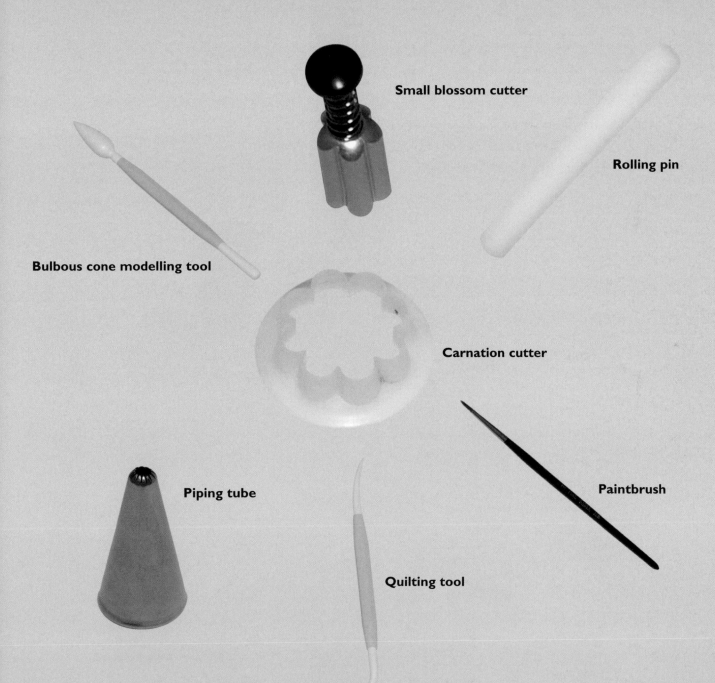

Small blossom cutter

Rolling pin

Bulbous cone modelling tool

Carnation cutter

Piping tube

Paintbrush

Quilting tool

Ingredients for models

All of these ingredients can be bought in advance and stored ready-to-use, apart from royal icing, which needs to be made up freshly when required and stored in an airtight bag.

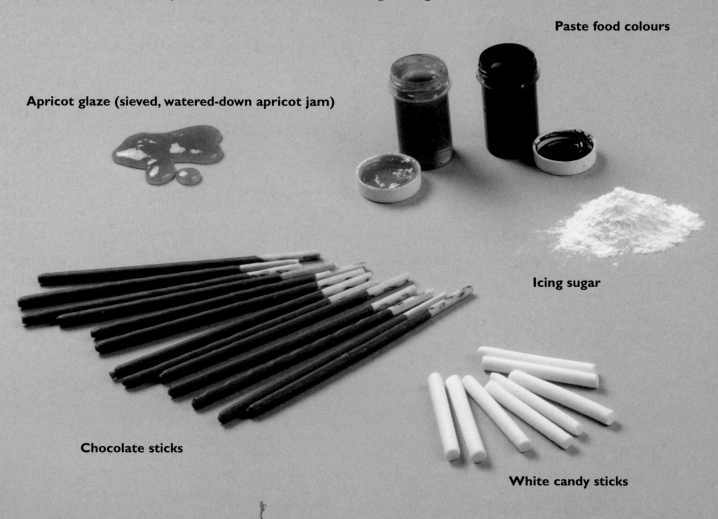

Paste food colours

Apricot glaze (sieved, watered-down apricot jam)

Icing sugar

Chocolate sticks

White candy sticks

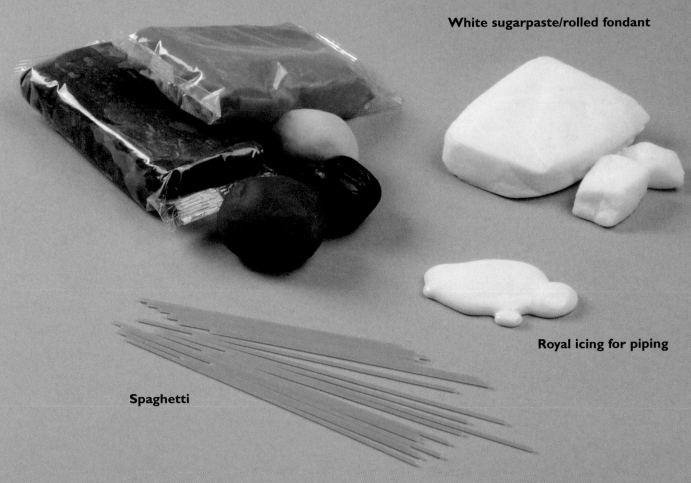

Coloured sugarpaste/rolled fondant

White sugarpaste/rolled fondant

Royal icing for piping

Spaghetti

Sugarpaste

This is sometimes referred to as 'fondant' or 'roll-out' icing. It is easily bought in sugarcraft shops and supermarkets. It is available in white and many different colours. Using ready-coloured paste can save a lot of time, especially with darker colours such as red, green or black.

Tip

If you wish to colour your own sugarpaste icing, use paste colours in preference to powder or liquid colours. Powder colours can create a grainy effect and liquid colours can change the consistency of your sugarpaste and make it sticky.

Colouring sugarpaste/royal icing

If you cannot buy readymade sugarpaste in the colour you require, buy white sugarpaste and colour it yourself. Use paste colours for best results as they are more concentrated and give deeper, richer colours. Royal icing is coloured in the same way.

1 Make a hole with your thumb in the middle of the piece of paste to be coloured. Dip a cocktail stick or toothpick into your chosen colour, then put the colour into the hole.

2 Fold the paste over and start to knead the colour in, using icing (confectioner's) sugar to prevent it sticking to the work surface or to your hands. Add more colour as necessary to achieve the colour you require, but take care not to add too much.

Paste colours you will need

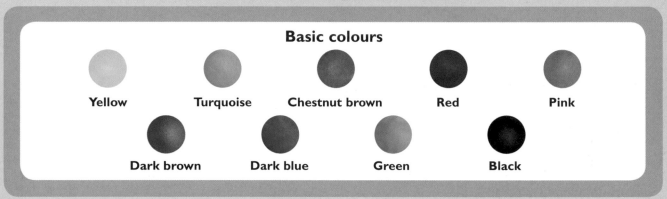

Basic colours

Yellow · Turquoise · Chestnut brown · Red · Pink

Dark brown · Dark blue · Green · Black

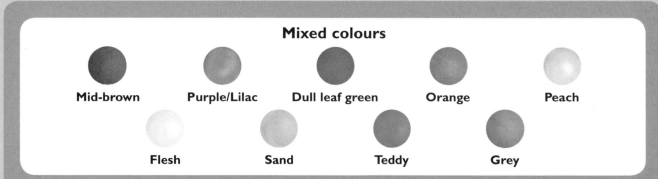

Mixed colours

Mid-brown · Purple/Lilac · Dull leaf green · Orange · Peach

Flesh · Sand · Teddy · Grey

To achieve:	Mix:
Mid-brown:	Chestnut brown and dark brown
Orange:	Yellow and red
Sand:	Orange, yellow and brown + lots of white sugarpaste
Purple/lilac:	Pink and blue
Peach:	Pink and yellow + white sugarpaste
Teddy':	Orange and brown + white sugarpaste
Dull leaf green:	Green and brown
Flesh:	Pink and yellow (tiny amounts of each) + lots of white sugarpaste
Grey:	Tiny amount of black mixed with white sugarpaste

Covering a cake and board

1 Sandwich your cake with the filling of your choice, then spread thinly all over with butter cream.

2 Roll out the sugarpaste to a thickness of ⅛in (3mm) on a surface dusted with icing sugar. Bring your cake as near to the rolled-out icing as possible, wrap the icing over your rolling pin, gently placing it on the cake.

3 Gently smooth the icing around the top edge of your cake using the palms of your hands.

4 Work your way smoothly down the sides of your cake until you reach the base.

5 Use a smoother in circular motions to gently 'polish' the top of the cake, flatten the top and create a sheen on the surface of your icing.

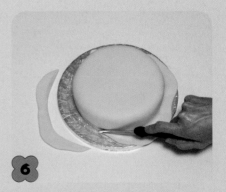

6 Using small cuts trim the icing off around the bottom of your cake.

Always place your cake on a board at least 2in (5cm) larger than the cake. If you use a much larger board, you can bring some models down on to the board too, for a more effective finished design.

7 Use the smoother around the sides of your cake to create beautifully straight sides.

8 Your cake is now ready to finish. To cover the silver board edge, follow the next four stages.

9 Brush on a very thin layer of water or apricot glaze.

10 Roll out a strip of sugarpaste. Cut a straight edge on one side and wrap it around the silver board, adding additional strips until the board edge is covered.

11 Trim all around the edge with little cuts, wipe your knife frequently and continue until the icing is trimmed all the way round.

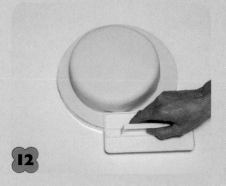

12 Smooth around the icing on the board, especially over the joins.

Covering a cake drum/board

Placing your models on a ready-iced cake drum or board is a brilliant idea if you want to keep them after the cake has been cut and eaten. If you use a thick drum cover the edge with a co-ordinating ribbon.

You will need

Cake drum
Pastry brush
Apricot glaze (see page 136)
Sugarpaste (see pages 138–39)

 1 Thinly brush the top of your board or cake drum with apricot glaze.

 2 Roll out your piece of sugarpaste to a ⅛in (3mm) thickness, place over your board and roll over with your rolling pin.

 3 Trim around the edge with small cuts, clean the blade of your knife frequently.

4 Your iced board is now ready to decorate.

How to mark eyes

You will need

Cocktail stick or toothpick
Black paste colour

Dip the end of your cocktail stick (or toothpick) into black paste colour and, following the instructions below, mark the eyes.

Do not mark the eyes as dots

Never push a cocktail stick or toothpick into the front of the face as this will form a little round eye and your model will look mean or unfriendly.

Mark oval or long eyes

Rest the black tip of the cocktail stick against the face to mark the eyes, approaching the head at the angle shown in the picture to ensure that the eyes are long, rather than round dots.

Compare the two faces

The one with long eyes (left) is much more friendly and appealing than the one with dot eyes (right).

Making a piping bag

You will need

Greaseproof or silicone paper

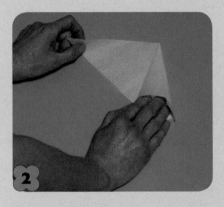

1 Cut a piece of greaseproof or silicone paper into a long triangle with one corner cut off. If right-handed, have this corner on your right, if left-handed have it on your left.

2 Pick up the right hand corner and twist it inwards until a tight point is formed in the middle of the long side.

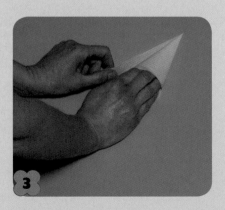

3 Rotate your hand inside until you have rolled to the end of the triangle and your cone is complete.

4 Bend the point of the paper inwards and tuck firmly into the cone.

5 Make a little rip halfway along, then fold over and bend one side inwards – this will secure the bag and stop it unravelling when you let go of it.

Making royal icing for piping

Royal icing is used for piping hair and piping grass, and it's also great for making little snowy patches on your Christmas scenes, or sticking your models to your cake.

You will need

3 fl oz (90ml) albumen solution (reconstituted egg white)
1lb/3 cups (500g) icing sugar, sifted
1 teaspoon glycerine
Colouring (if required – see 'Colouring sugarpaste/royal Icing', pages 138–39)

Put all the ingredients together in a bowl and beat with an electric mixer on slow speed until peaked consistency is achieved.

Tip
When storing royal icing, always cover it with a damp cloth, or put in a sealed container to prevent it drying out.

Piping hair and grass

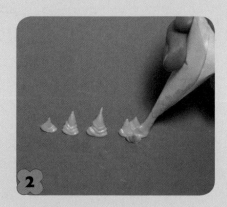

1 Colour your royal icing and fill one third of your piping bag. Fold the open end of the bag over several times, flatten the pointed end, then cut the end as shown.

2 Gently squeeze a blob of icing out of the bag, stop squeezing and pull away and you will have formed a little spike of grass or hair.

Men's hair

1 Three little spikes on each side of the head will make the Clown's hair.

2 Add a row of spikes along the back of the head for the Mechanic's hair.

3 Fill in the top of the head and pipe a fringe for the Man's and Toddler's hair.

4 To make someone look younger add a few long spikes on top of their head.

Santa Claus's hair

Note:
Place a small star tube in the end of a paper bag and one-third fill with white royal icing.

1 Squeeze a few spikes of hair each side of the top of the head and a line around the back, leave the top bald.

2 Start to pipe hair down his cheeks and across his chin to form a beard.

3 Finally pipe two long spikes of icing under his nose and pull one to the right and one to the left to make a big moustache.

Women's hair

1 Fill a third of your bag with pale yellow royal icing, then cut the end off the bag as illustrated.

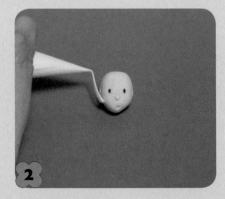

2 Squeeze and attach a large blob of icing to the side of the lady's face and pull it upwards.

3 Finish piping at the top of the head, and pull away.

4 Repeat this action all around the back of the head. If the icing finishes with spikes at the top of the head allow the royal icing to dry for a few minutes – then pat the spikes down to create a smoother finish.

5 Continue piping around the other side of the face until the hairstyle is completed.

Making an armchair

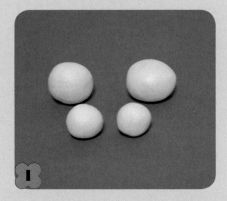

1 Form all the ball shapes in your chosen colour.

2 Flatten them a little.

3 Stick the back and base together at a right angle, press together firmly to stick.

4 Press the two smaller balls each side for the arms of the chair.

Part	Template
Back	2 x A mixed together
Base	2 x A mixed together
Arms	2 x B

See templates for sizes on page 133

Making a Christmas tree

You will need

Sugarpaste (required amount)
Pointed-end tool
Pair of small nail scissors
Icing sugar for snow

1 Form any size ball of sugarpaste into a pointed cone.

2 Place the cone on to the pointed end of the tool. Rest a small pair of open nail scissors against the side of the cone near the top and snip the icing to form a branch.

3 Revolve the cone and cut all around the top of the tree, then move downwards and cut all around the next layer.

4 Continue until you reach the bottom of the tree, making larger cuts for the lower branches.

5 Make your trees in green or white and sprinkle with icing sugar for snow.

About the author

Ann Pickard qualified as a Baker and Cake Decorator in 1983 and opened her own shop, 'The Icing Centre', in 1986. She runs a successful cake-decorating business in Weston-super-Mare in Somerset, UK and has published seven books on cake decorating, called *The Idiot's Guides*, which have sold in excess of 45,000 copies in the last 16 years. She has also produced a range of DVDs on the same subject.

Dedication

Many thanks to Dave and Jane for all your help.

Acknowledgement

Many thanks to Renshaw, for supplying the Regalice sugarpaste for this book.

Photographic acknowledgements

All photographs by Nick Sparks, except those on pp.136–37, GMC/Anthony Bailey.

Suppliers

UK

Sugarpaste

COVA PASTE: white sugarpaste
BFP Wholesale Ltd
Unit 8 Connections Industrial Centre
Vestry Road
Sevenoaks
TN14 5DF
enquiries@bfpwholesale.com

ICECRAFT: white sugarpaste
British Sugar plc
Sugar Way
Peterborough
PE2 9AY
Tel: +44 (0)1733 563171
www.britishsugar.co.uk

www.bfpwholesale.com
REGALICE: white and coloured sugarpaste
Renshaw
Crown Street
Liverpool
L8 7RF
Tel: +44 (0)151 706 8200
www.renshawnapier.co.uk

Sugarcraft equipment

Culpitt Ltd
Jubilee Industrial Estate
Ashington
Northumberland
NE63 8UQ
Tel: +44 (0) 1670 814545
www.culpitt.com

Guy Paul and Co Ltd
Unit 10 The Business Centre
Corinium Industrial Estate
Raans Road
Amersham
Bucks
HP6 6FB
Tel: +44 (0)1494 432121
www.guypaul.co.uk

Knightsbridge PME
Chadwell Heath Lane
Romford
Essex
RM6 4NP
Tel: +44 (0)20 8590 5959
www.cakedecoration.co.uk

US

Sugarcraft equipment

Beryl's Cake Decorating & Pastry Supplies
PO Box 1584
North Springfield, VA 22151
U.S.A.
www.beryls.com

Sugarcraft™
3665 Dixie Hwy
Hamilton, OH 45015
U.S.A.
www.sugarcraft.com

AUSTRALIA

Sugarcraft equipment

Bakery Sugarcraft
198 Newton Road
Wetherill Park
NSW 2164
Australia
www.bakerysugarcraft.com.au

Index

A

animal fur/hair
  large dog 61
  lion's mane 68
  mole skin 88
  pony's mane 73
  rabbit's fur 20
  small dog 41
  teddy fur 13
  wool on sheep 45
  zebra's mane 81
apricot glaze 136
armchair 149

B

Baby 119–21
blanket 13
blossom cutter 135
bulbous cone modelling tool 135
bulrushes 29

C

cake-boards 141, 142
car wheels 128
carnation cutter 135
Cat 51–3
Christmas tree 150
Clown 123–5, 146
cocktail stick 134
coloured sugarpaste 137
colouring sugarpaste/royal icing 138
colours 139
covering a cake 140–1
covering cake boards 141, 142
covering a cake drum 142
crimper 134
Crocodile 83–5

D

dogs see Large dogs; Small dogs
Donkey 75–7
Ducks 27–9

E

Elephant 15–17
equipment 134–5
Eskimo 99–101
eyes, marking 14

F

fishing rod 105
fondant 137, 138
Frog 31–3

G

grass 29, 69, 145

H

hair 145
  men's 146
  Santa Claus's 147
  women's 148
  see also animal fur/hair

I

icing 137
  colouring 138
  making 145
icing sugar 136
ingredients 136–7

K

knife 134

L

Large dog 59–61

Lion 67–9

M

Man in chair 111–13, 146

Mechanic 127–9, 146

mixing colours 139

Mole 87–9

Monkey 55–7

Mouse 35–7

N

newspaper 113

P

paintbrush 135

paste colours 136, 138

Penguins 23–5

Pig 47–9

piping bags 134, 144

piping tube 135

Polar bear 103–5

Pony 71–3

Q

quilting tool 135

R

Rabbits

blue 19, 20–1

brown 19, 21

rolled fondant 137

rolling pin 135

royal icing 137

colouring 138

making 145

storing 145

ruffled texture 13

ruffles (on clown) 124

S

Santa Claus 95–7, 147, 150

scissors 134

Sheep 43–5

Small dogs

brown 39, 40

white 39, 41

Snowman 91–3

spaghetti 137

for bulrushes 29

sugarpaste 137

sugarpaste templates 133

suppliers 153

T

Teddy 11–13

templates 133

Tiger 63–5

Toddler 115–17

tools 134–5

W

white candy sticks 136

white sugarpaste 137

Woman in chair 107–9, 148–9

Z

Zebra 79–81

To place an order, or to request a catalogue, contact:

GMC Publications Ltd

Castle Place, 166 High Street, Lewes, East Sussex, BN7 1XU

United Kingdom

Tel: 01273 488005   **Fax:** 01273 402866

Website: www.gmcbooks.com

Orders by credit card are accepted